Praise for
Stand-Up Guys

"*Stand-Up Guys* is a delightful survey of godly men throughout history, a much-needed easy reference of models for the next generation to learn from."

KEVAN CHANDLER, author of *We Carry Kevan*

"I love what Kate and Caroline have done with this collection of stories! Each chapter shines a light on a world changer, a role model I would want my kids to look up to. It's so important for young people to see how God can use anybody to do great things. And this book shines a bright light on fifty individuals who have lived their lives for a greater cause. I pray the stories Kate and Caroline have told here will light a fire in the hearts of our next generation's stand-up guys and girls."

MATTHEW WEST, Grammy-nominated and Dove Award-winning singer, songwriter, and author

"What a delightful book, with insight about both little-known and iconic men who changed the world around them. A great way to learn about historic figures while garnering inspiration for how to conquer obstacles to achieve the goals you have today."

CINDY MORGAN, singer/songwriter at www.cindymorganmusic.com

"More than ever, we need books that celebrate honorable men who have lived by their faith. This book couldn't come at a better time to speak to the hearts of the next generation."

JAMIE SUMNER, author of the middle grade novel *Roll with It* and the faith-based parenting books *Eat, Sleep, Save the World* and *Unbound*

"Like all great books for kids and teens, *Stand-Up Guys* is equally beneficial for grown-ups. Each short biography provides meaningful inspiration from one of history's great influencers, and much more. Each man's story is revealed to be part of the bigger Story of God, with takeaway questions for parents and kids to consider together. What a great resource! What Kate and Caroline have provided here will both instruct and inspire."

SCOTT SAULS, senior pastor of Christ Presbyterian Church and author of several books, including *Jesus Outside the Lines* and *Irresistible Faith*

"In an era when the shocking and appalling populate our pixels, *Stand-Up Guys* offers a helpful alternative for young readers, demonstrating the profound power of simple faithfulness. This book reminds that whatever talents the Lord has given, they are to be used with faithfulness to extend His kingdom."

BETH GRAHAM, Assistant Director of Spiritual Development,
Christ Presbyterian Academy (Nashville, TN)

"*Stand-Up Guys* is a must for your homeschool library. This book of mini biographies disrupts 'comfortable Christianity' with simple yet direct challenges to live radically and globally."

GINA MUNSEY, writer and creator of Oaxacaborn.com

"The author of the book of Hebrews writes, 'Since we are surrounded by so great a cloud of witnesses, let us also lay aside every weight and the sin that clings so closely … and run with perseverance' (Hebrews 12:1). In every generation, Christians—particularly our boys— must remember those who have blazed the trail before us. History is full of great examples of Christian men. *Stand-Up Guys* pulls fifty role models who didn't take the easy or expected path but fought to shape and change the world for the glory of Christ. May this book inspire a new generation of young people to love the Lord without regard for self."

CHRISTOPHER YUAN, DMin, speaker and author of *Out of a Far Country: A Gay Son's Journey to God, A Broken Mother's Search for Hope* and *Holy Sexuality and the Gospel: Sex, Desire, and Relationships Shaped by God's Grand Story*

"I love this book!! It's a great book because it gives a history lesson that isn't boring."

JON ADAIR, age 13

STAND-UP GUYS

50 CHRISTIAN MEN WHO CHANGED THE WORLD

KATE ETUE & CAROLINE SIEGRIST

ZONDERkidz

ZONDERKIDZ

Stand-Up Guys
Copyright © 2020 by Katharine A. Etue and Caroline Siegrist

Requests for information should be addressed to:
Zonderkidz, *3900 Sparks Dr. SE, Grand Rapids, Michigan 49546*

Hardcover ISBN 978-0-310-76970-5

Ebook ISBN 978-0-310-76971-2

Interior design: Denise Froehlich
Interior illustrations: Matthew Taylor Wilson

Printed in China

20 21 22 23 24 /DSC/ 10 9 8 7 6 5 4 3 2 1

for
Jackson
Grey
Annie
Hayes
and **Maggie**

contents

INTRODUCTION

What do you think it means to be a Christian? Some say it means always being nice, always being good. But if you look at the life of Jesus, you'll see that loving God means you sometimes must be daring, adventurous, and bold. Sometimes, we're asked to love people so radically it can even be . . . dangerous.

When we chose the men to include in this book, we thought about that type of love. We wanted to find men who lived interesting, unusual lives. Men who didn't take the expected path. Men who dared to face danger so they could love others as God loved them.

You don't have to be a pastor to change the world (although you can if that's what you want to do!). Like the men in this book, you can be a surfer, an artist, a filmmaker, a basketball player, a politician, a scientist, or anything else that excites you and still make a difference.

Even though all the people in this book are men, we know that any boy *or* girl reading these stories can be adventurous and brave. The world needs kids like you to grow up loving God and fighting to make this a better place to live.

So be brave, love others, and be a stand-up kid. We can't wait to see how you're going to change the world too.

xo, Kate and Caroline

EDDIE AIKAU

1946–1978 • Hawaii

When the sun rose over the ocean on the Kahului Harbor beach in Maui, you could often find Eddie Aikau wading out into the water with his surfboard. Being in the ocean was his passion, and he felt most alive when he was surfing the biggest waves Hawaii had to offer. Even the thirty-footers weren't too big for him.

Eddie grew up with a mindset to serve others—whether he was ministering as a church altar boy or being a great older brother to his siblings. Eddie wanted the best for others. Eventually he became the first lifeguard at Waimea Beach in Hawaii. He was absolutely dedicated to his job, and he ultimately rescued five hundred people from drowning in the strong currents and powerful waves. Even more remarkable, not one person—not one—died while Eddie was on watch. No matter how rough the waters were, Eddie was always willing to risk his life to save someone who was drowning.

Eddie felt it was important to do whatever it took to save relationships too. During one competition, Australian surfer Rabbit Bartholomew made the Hawaiian surfing community angry by acting like he and his fellow surfers invented the sport. Things got really tense and a huge fistfight broke out—there were even death threats. But Eddie invited the Australian surfers to reconcile with the Hawaiian surfers in a traditional *ho'oponopono*—the Hawaiian custom of putting things right in a family meeting. They were able to come to an agreement about their competitive relationship.

In 1978, Eddie was invited to participate in an old-school Polynesian voyage on vintage rafts like his ancestors would have used. Once they were out at sea, the crew encountered treacherous water and the boat capsized. Of course, Eddie immediately offered to paddle for help. But while the Coast Guard was rescuing the other men, Eddie disappeared. He was never seen again.

Eddie's gravestone reads, "Greater love has no one than this: to lay down one's life for one's friends" (John 15:13), because he died just as he lived, risking his own life to save others.

- Have you ever let fear keep you from helping others?
- What brave thing could you do today to help fix a broken friendship?

JOSÉ ANDRÉS

Born 1969 • Spain

José Andrés had just $50 in his pocket when he stepped off the plane from Barcelona, a twenty-one-year-old in Manhattan and on his own for the first time. He had a burning passion to share Spanish food with the people of New York. It didn't take long for his enthusiasm to ignite the city and draw the attention of customers and restaurant owners.

Fast-forward twenty years, and José now owns more than thirty restaurants and is one of the most prominent chefs in the United States. He's won prestigious awards for his unique creations and the way he shared his Spanish culture with American diners.

José enjoys making new and exciting meals for people in his restaurants, but he knows that all around the world there are families with hungry children. In 2010, José remembered how Jesus multiplied only a few loaves and fish to feed thousands—and wondered if he could do something similar with his cooking skills. So he formed a nonprofit called World Central Kitchen, which mobilizes chefs to provide healthy, fresh meals to the survivors of natural disasters—kind of like Doctors without Borders, but for food.

When Hurricane Maria hit Puerto Rico, José Andrés knew that was where God wanted him to be. The whole island was hungry. People had no food, no power, and no shelter. His first day there, José and his team fed one thousand people. The day after that, they fed five thousand. Instead of eating prepackaged, ready-to-eat meals, the tired, scared hurricane survivors were able to enjoy hot chicken and rice prepared by a world-famous chef. As word began to spread around the island, more and more people came to eat his food.

Luckily, chefs are great at handling chaos. José and his team converted a nearby arena into a massive kitchen and started cooking even more food for people in need. Within a few weeks, the team was serving up almost 150,000 meals a day.

As an immigrant to the United States, José worked hard to achieve his dream of owning a restaurant. But now he says he believes the real American dream is working hard to help others, which is more important than any cooking award.

- How can you use your skills to help others?
- What do you think it means to be "successful"?

francis of assisi

1181–1226 • Italy

Francis was the guy everyone wanted at their party, and when he was young he wasn't exactly a "saint." He was born into a wealthy family, with every advantage in life. In addition to being rich, Francis was handsome, smart, and charming. If he lived today, he probably would have been an Instagram influencer.

As much as Francis loved the luxuries in his life, he felt a longing for something more. Thinking that taking part in a high-stakes battle might scratch that itch, Francis decided to try proving himself in the military. To be honest, he'd tried once before and ended up in an enemy prison for a year. Though this time, he decided to buy the finest armor and cloak money could buy. But the day after he rode off to join in the Crusades, God spoke to Francis, telling him to return home.

Ashamed, Francis rode back into town bearing the same shining armor—without a single scratch on it. Everyone ridiculed Francis for chickening out before he even got to the battle-field, but God had other plans for him.

Francis started hiding away in quiet places to pray. One day, when he was praying in a run-down church, he heard the voice of God telling him to "rebuild his church." Thinking God meant the physical church he was kneeling in, Francis went and sold some of his father's silks to raise money for repairs. But his father found out and was furious.

It took Francis a lot of prayer and solitude to realize that God might not be talking about that church in particular, but rather the whole Church—the family of believers living on earth. From that point, Francis gave away everything he owned, right down to his beautiful clothes, and decided to live in the forest with the creatures he loved.

- What do you want people to notice about you?
- What might God be asking you to give up in your life?

andrew van der bijl

Born 1928 • Netherlands

As his Volkswagen Beetle idled in place, Brother Andrew could feel his blood pressure rising. His hands felt clammy on the steering wheel as he watched officials at the border checkpoint order drivers to exit their vehicles and take out all their belongings. It was the 1950s in Communist Romania, and religious materials were strictly forbidden. But Andrew's car was packed full of Bibles. He could be thrown into prison if even one of them were discovered.

While growing up as a poor child in the Netherlands, Andrew van der Bijl never would have expected he'd become "God's Smuggler," risking his freedom (and maybe even his life) to transport illegal Bibles to Christians inside Communist countries. In fact, he wasn't even raised in the church. His blacksmith father and invalid mother did the best they could, but Andrew first learned about Jesus when he read the Bible as he was healing from an injury.

His passion for God's Word became an obsession.

Now, sitting in his car, Andrew knew that turning around would look very suspicious. His only option was to continue inching forward. He was sure there was no way he would make it through the inspection without the guards finding the Bibles stashed in his backseat.

Trembling with fear, Andrew prayed. God simply said, "Trust me." So instead of leaving them hidden, Andrew pulled a few of the Bibles out so they were clearly visible. He handed the guard his passport through the window, but the guard merely glanced at the document and waved him through. Just like that.

From that moment on, Andrew knew God was protecting him. It made him even bolder as he continued to smuggle illegal Bibles to parts of the world where people couldn't get them—and places where people had never heard the name of Jesus—for the next forty years.

Andrew proved that if you believe God's got your back, there's almost nothing you can't do.

- How has God helped you to be courageous?
- Have you ever had to break the rules to follow God?

DIETRICH BONHOEFFER

1906–1945 • Poland

Bombs squealed through the dark sky overhead, and the sound of warning sirens echoed off the buildings nearby. In the distance, bricks and pavement exploded in the night. But Dietrich Bonhoeffer simply tucked his head down and continued on his journey with increasing determination. There were Jewish people in this city to be saved, and it was up to him to save them.

Growing up, Dietrich went to church, but his family didn't make that big a deal about faith in their everyday lives. So when he decided to set aside his musical talent for a job studying the Bible, they were shocked.

This was at a time, however, when many German pastors were preaching that God wanted Hitler in charge of their country. To Dietrich, this was the farthest thing from the truth. Not surprisingly, the German government banned Dietrich from preaching publicly when he refused to support Hitler. So, he began an underground seminary where he trained pastors in secret instead. He taught them the idea that "comfortable Christianity" isn't real faith. Faith requires action. Sometimes uncomfortable, even dangerous action.

Despite his best efforts to convince German Christians to fight against their political leader, Hitler's power continued to rise—and Jewish people were captured, imprisoned, and killed. Dietrich decided it was time to do more.

He joined the German secret service so he could spy *against* them. He traveled to church conferences all over Europe, but instead of simply collecting information for the Germans, he would help Jews escape.

Eventually, a plot was hatched to assassinate Hitler. But Hitler survived. Furious that their leader had been attacked, the Nazis looked for anyone who had even the smallest connection to the plan. Dietrich had already been imprisoned for his role in the resistance against the German government, but once he was connected to the assassination, his fate was sealed. On April 9, 1945, Dietrich was executed at dawn at Flossenbürg concentration camp—just two weeks before US soldiers stormed the camp and liberated its prisoners.

Today, Dietrich Bonhoeffer is remembered as one of the smartest, bravest men of faith during World War II.

- Have you ever had to stand up to someone for what you believe?
- What does "comfortable Christianity" look like to a kid your age?

BONO

Born 1960 • Ireland

When he was fourteen years old, Paul Hewson stood in an Irish cemetery as his grandfather's body was lowered into the earth. His mother cried nearby as he pushed his hands into his pockets to stay warm. He wondered how his life could get any worse.

But then it did. Paul's mother, overcome by her sadness, collapsed to the ground. Paul watched helplessly as she was rushed to a nearby hospital, but it was too late.

In just a few days, Paul had lost his mother and his grandfather. His house, once cheerful, was now filled with grief and anger. Paul could have turned to many things to ease the pain of his grief—many things that weren't good for him—but instead he turned to music.

Soon, Paul and a few friends started a band, and before long he had a new name: Bono. Since then, Bono has skyrocketed to stardom with his band U2. Many of their songs that center around protest—against apartheid, against the Protestant-Catholic violence in Dublin, and against injustices around the world—are what they're best known for. It's been his way of speaking truth to a broken world.

But Bono's faith told him that just being a "good voice" wasn't enough. God wanted him to go out and see what he was doing around the world, so Bono could get involved in God's work. So Bono and his wife, Ali, traveled to Ethiopia to volunteer at an orphanage. There, many people were sick—and going to die—from a preventable disease called AIDS, just because they were poor.

Bono started meeting with pastors and politicians around the world. He convinced them to send money and supplies, and to forgive the money African countries owed so that they could spend it taking care of their own citizens instead.

Bono has spent more than twenty years fighting for a healthier Africa. He's even been nominated for a Nobel Peace Prize for all he's done to help the poor.

- Do you use art or music (or something else) to express yourself when you're sad or scared?
- How can you support the causes you care about?

NOrman Borlaug

1914–2009 • United States

In the 1960s, scientists predicted chronic food shortages around the globe. More than a billion people would die of starvation if the problem wasn't solved. But when plant scientist Norman Borlaug arrived in Mexico, he didn't have much hope a solution would be found. The Mexican farmers were working poor soil that didn't yield enough wheat to feed their families, much less turn a profit. Plus, the farmers were resistant to trying any new growing techniques, especially when they came from a stranger who didn't even speak their language.

Norman had already spent hours in the lab working to develop a wheat variety that resisted rust, a disease that caused the plants to wither. But this new wheat didn't have a strong enough stem, so it fell over and stopped growing when it got too heavy.

Then he had a brilliant idea. He'd crossbreed his weak but rust-resistant wheat with one that was shorter, with a sturdier stem. He and his team of young scientists traveled back and forth to Mexico to perfect the new crop in the hot, dry climate where the farmers lived. And he worked hard to learn Spanish so he could communicate with them in their own language.

Norman's new miracle seeds enabled the farmers to feed more and more people. He had almost single-handedly prevented the starvation crisis in Mexico, as well as other places in the world.

And he found that when people were able to feed themselves, all kinds of other problems were solved too. When they had full bellies, people were less likely to wage war against each other. The children were healthier and stayed in school longer. Across the board, their lives dramatically improved.

In his Nobel Prize acceptance speech, Norman Borlaug said he hoped that his wheat would make the prophesies in Isaiah come true. He longed for the day when the "parched ground shall become a pool, and the thirsty land springs of water."

And his seeds are helping that dream come true, even today. It's estimated that Norman Borlaug has saved a billion lives with his "miracle seeds." Not bad for a farm boy from Iowa.

- How can your curiosity about the natural world serve God and other people?
- How can you help fight hunger in your own community?

George Washington Carver

1864–1943 • United States

On a dusty dirt road in Diamond, Missouri, a group of men hurried out of town, looking over their shoulders as they traveled. In their posse was a kidnapped slave woman and her baby boy, frightened for their lives.

Eventually, a Union scout rescued the young boy, but his mother had vanished. The child was returned to his owners, Moses and Susan Carver, who took him in and raised him, even after slavery was abolished. His name was George.

George Washington Carver had an incredible mind and was fascinated by everything he saw in nature. He once said he believed nature was God's broadcasting system, the way he speaks to us, and he wanted to learn everything God was telling him. So at age eleven, he left home and set out to study, supporting himself by washing clothes for people. Finally, after years of hard work, he received an advanced degree at the top of his class.

George refused to use his brilliant mind only for personal gain. He saw the struggles of poor farmers in the South, who reminded him of Moses Carver. The soil on their farms was basically dead; it had almost no nutrients to support the plants they were trying to grow.

George set to work researching. He and his students hauled mud from a nearby swamp to help restore the worn-out soil. They also realized the cotton and corn that nearly every Southern farmer grew did not give needed nutrients back into the soil. As a result, he suggested they rotate their regular crops with new ones that would give the soil better nutrients. Problem solved! But a new problem arose—no one wanted to buy the peanuts, sweet potatoes, and soybeans they were now growing.

So George did even more research. He ultimately discovered more than one hundred uses for the everyday peanut, which meant the farmers could now sell more of them and make more money, bringing their families out of poverty.

- Are you feeling bored with your life? What could you rotate out for a season so you can try something new?
- What are the life-giving activities or people in your life that help you feel nourished and healthy?

steven curtis chapman

Born 1962 • United States

As Steven and Mary Beth Chapman dodged traffic and shuffled around street vendors, they realized just how far they were from their home in Tennessee. They'd arrived in China and were heading into one of the great adventures of their lives, filled with nervous excitement.

This story had started years earlier, when they took their daughter Emily on a missions trip to Haiti. They'd hoped Emily would see a side of life that didn't include the level of privilege she'd grown up with as the child of one of Christian music's biggest stars.

But they didn't expect the passion that ignited in her would lead their family to adopt three precious girls—Shaoey, Stevey Joy, and Maria—from China. Which was why they were heading to a Chinese courthouse that day.

For years, Steven had sung about following God in his hit song "The Great Adventure": "Let's follow our Leader into the glorious unknown. This is the life like no other. This is the great adventure." God's promise to place orphans in families became one of Steven's life's passions, and he could see a new chapter of his adventure unfolding. He and his wife started an organization called Show Hope. Even when couples are willing to adopt, sometimes they can't afford the thousands of dollars in fees. That's where Show Hope comes in, offering money to help cover their expenses.

But God wasn't done with Steven's adventure, and he continued to listen to God's voice. His journey took him back to China and inspired him to build a huge, six-story home for orphans, painted bright blue with big white clouds on it. It's called Maria's Big House of Hope.

More than two hundred children with special needs live there, and they get medical care and lots of love while they wait to be adopted.

Isn't it amazing to see where God can take you, if only you're willing to listen to and follow his voice? It really is a great adventure, isn't it?

- What is one small (or big) way you and your family could help care for orphans?
- What's the most daring, adventurous thing you can imagine God asking you to do to help others?

cecil chaudhry

1941–2012 • Pakistan

On a balmy August morning in the Salt Range of Punjab, British India, the only Catholic family in town celebrated the birth of their new baby boy. In an area of the world that was nearly torn apart because of rifts between Hindus and Muslims, the Chaudhry family had lived alone as Christians for many years. They had no idea that their new son, Cecil, would become an important figure in uniting not only his community but his entire country.

Just two weeks before Cecil's sixth birthday, his Muslim-majority country declared independence from Hindu-majority India. Young Cecil took advantage of every opportunity this new country had to offer. He joined the Royal Pakistan Air Force in order to become a pilot, and the next year he was piloting glider planes. When the president of Pakistan gave him an award, he knew he'd spend the rest of his life flying.

Cecil was good at it too. After fighting in two different wars to defend his country, he was declared a hero. Even still, anti-Christian prejudice in his Muslim-run country hurt him. In fact, he believed he—and other Christians—were passed over for better jobs simply because of their faith.

Instead of whining about it, Cecil decided to do something. After his retirement from the military, he worked tirelessly toward equality for all people in Pakistan. And when we say tirelessly, we mean he woke up regularly at 4:00 a.m. to have enough time to do everything he wanted to in a day.

Part of this work was improving Pakistani national schools. Their schoolbooks ignored the important contributions of minority members of his society. By telling the history of *all* people of Pakistan, he believed they would become a more united country.

Today, his daughter continues his mission to fight against racism. She helps people in practical ways, like paying bills for medical treatment or education for kids who are victims of extremist violence. In this way they are loving their community the way Jesus loved his.

- How can you make your community more inclusive to all types of people?
- What do you think it would be like to grow up as a Christian in a country where Christians are a significant minority?

samuel Ajayi crowther

1809–1891 • Nigeria

Ajayi and his family were beginning their breakfast when raiders attacked his African village. Just thirteen years old, he and his mother and siblings scrambled to escape, but it was too late. The invaders tracked them down before they got far from their home. Before he knew it, there was a thick rope around his neck and his freedom was stolen.

Ajayi changed hands six times as the slave traders bid and bargained. Eventually, he was put on a Portuguese slave ship bound for Europe, but before the ship reached its destination, the British navy stopped it and demanded the release of every slave.

Ajayi was relieved, but he had no idea where he would end up next. Ultimately, the British sailors dropped him off in Sierra Leone, a Christian colony founded by abolitionists (people fighting against slavery) and freed slaves.

Before long, Ajayi was able to start school in his new home. His teachers quickly noticed his talent for learning languages. And another important thing happened: Ajayi heard about Jesus for the first time. When he was baptized, he gave himself a new name: Samuel Crowther, after one of the founders of the church mission society.

A few years later, Samuel was recruited for a mission to Niger (now Nigeria). He and the other missionaries wanted to help spread the Christian faith and destroy the slave trade. Thanks to his leadership, he was soon invited to be ordained as a minister.

Samuel believed that slavery could only be destroyed when Africans developed their own economy. He taught new farming techniques, preached the gospel, and helped build trade with other countries—of goods, not people. Samuel translated the whole Bible into the Yoruba language because he didn't want to force his fellow Nigerians to learn English in order to know about God. Samuel was named the first African bishop in the Anglican church, and he continued to support his people until the day he died.

- Who do you think of as an oppressed group? How can you help defend their rights?
- Did you know there are still twenty-five million enslaved people around the world today? What could you do to help end modern-day slavery?

KUNIYAL KANDI DEVARAJ

Born 1952 • India

The streets of Mumbai are packed with cars, mopeds, people, and even the occasional cow. A mobile food truck driver honks his horn as he tries to turn onto a side street leading to one of the poorer parts of town. When he sees the familiar, dirty faces of the homeless children he's met there, he pulls over and waves.

The kids crowd the van, smiling and reaching out for their lunches. This mobile meal delivery service is just one of the life-changing ideas that Kuniyal "KK" Devaraj came up with over the years to help his neighbors.

Like most people in India, KK was born to an orthodox Hindu family. But when he met Jesus, it changed his life. He wanted to make the world a better place for the poor, so he left his good job behind and moved to Mumbai. There, he purposely found a place to live in the dodgy part of town, near criminals and drug addicts. He wanted to help the kids who lived there.

His first step was to create a daycare where kids could stay so they'd be off the streets while their parents worked. But he noticed that many of the women in his neighborhood worked at night in an area called the red-light district. It was terrible work, made worse by the fact their children were left alone overnight.

KK decided to open a night shelter where kids could safely be cared for. He started a school so daughters would receive an education and not have to follow in their moms' footsteps. And for the women who were able to leave the red-light district, he started a community called Ashagram, which means "Village of Hope." There, abused women find shelter, counseling, and simply the chance to have fun.

KK says that Jesus calls his children "expensive pearls," and just because a pearl has a little dirt on it, it's no less valuable. Our job as Christians is to help hurting people find their chance to shine again.

- Do you know any people in your church or school who could use some hope? How could you help?
- How does it feel to know Jesus thinks of you as an expensive pearl?

TONY DUNGY

Born 1955 • United States

Right from the start, Tony Dungy stood out among the other NFL coaches. He didn't scream until his face turned red or play favorites with the stars on his team. He saw himself as a teacher first, and he wanted to treat his players according to his Christian faith.

Soon his unusual approach started to show success. By 1996, Tony was hired as head coach for the Buccaneers, who were struggling to have a winning season. Tony used his signature kindness-first teaching and defensive skills knowledge to turn the team around. Within a few years, the team had a winning record again.

Tony was soon scooped up by another team, the Indianapolis Colts. He quickly helped strengthen their weak defense, and the team immediately began performing better. In October 2005, he signed a three-year contract for $5 million a year.

Everything was looking up for Tony.

But that December, something unimaginable happened. Tony received a call in the middle of the night from a police officer. His oldest son had committed suicide.

Tony couldn't believe it. His mind was racing with questions. He was angry and sad. Coaching was the last thing he felt like doing.

But a week later, Tony got back on the field. He'd always taught his players about resilience—the ability to bounce back—and now it was time to model it firsthand. Tony continued coaching his team, and in 2007 he became the first African American coach to win the Super Bowl—a lifelong dream.

But the ache in his heart wasn't gone. He missed his son terribly, and he didn't want any other parent to experience that trauma. So he began speaking openly about his son's death to help raise awareness of mental health issues among kids. He wanted kids to know that if they're feeling suicidal too, they should tell someone they love.

Tony found that his coaching skills helped people off the field as well, and he's helped many people find peace and comfort with Jesus.

- How can you use kindness to help you accomplish your goals?
- How can you use a loss or hardship in your life to help others?

HOWARD FINSTER

1916–2001 • United States

Howard Finster dipped his finger into the bucket of white paint and started painting the bicycle he was fixing. He was the pastor of a small local church, but it wasn't quite paying the bills, so he took on a lot of odd jobs like this one to support his wife and five kids. As he pulled his finger away from the bike and looked down, he gasped.

On the pad of his finger was a perfect human face. Whose face? He had no idea. But in the same moment, he felt a warmth spread over his body and he heard the words, "Paint sacred art." He knew it was God speaking to him.

Still, Howard couldn't help arguing. Just a little. "I can't do that," he said. He told God he didn't have an ounce of artistic training. But God wasn't letting him win the argument.

So Howard starting drawing. And painting. And before he knew it, he was also creating a sculpture park in his backyard using scraps of old bicycles and televisions—basically anything he could find. Before long, people from all around the Southeast were coming to see his backyard, which was soon dubbed "Paradise Gardens."

Howard also found that making art was a great way to convey the spiritual messages he had learned. Where people might forget his sermons hours after they heard them, they could continue to look at one of his paintings day after day.

Before he knew it, Howard's art was being featured in places like the Smithsonian and the Library of Congress. Popular bands like R.E.M. and the Talking Heads wanted to use his paintings on their album covers. Before he died, Howard said leaving your talents undiscovered was like leaving milk to spoil. He encouraged people everywhere to get their hands dirty and get creative. After all, you'll never know what masterpieces you've got in you until you try.

- What's one way you can practice creativity today?
- Has God been calling you to do something, but you've been scared to try? How can you make a small step in that direction today?

Matt Hall

Born 1990 • United States

The chaplain's patch on his backpack was the only way Matt Hall would stand out among the other hikers on the trail as he took his first steps into the woods in Maine. Hiking wasn't Matt's passion, but here he was, setting off on a six-month journey over 2,190 miles of cool, dense forest, heart-stopping mountain views, and day-after-day monotony on the Appalachian Trail.

Matt had been thinking about working as a pastor, but his heart told him to look for a job that would help him meet people from different backgrounds. He wasn't sure that's what he'd find in his small-town Tennessee church. So when a friend told him about this unusual way to serve God, he took a leap of faith and applied for the job.

Matt's rebellious teen years didn't make him a typical pastor, but his new job was anything but typical. He was to simply be a friend to the people he met along the trail. And, as it turned out, many of the people he met needed one.

It seemed like every hiker he met was experiencing change. Maybe they were going from college to a job for the first time, or they had lost someone they loved, or they'd been recently released from jail. Knowing that Matt—and God—accepted them as they were really helped.

While out in nature for that long, not distracted by screens and the busyness of life, Matt realized his faith could be a lot simpler than he'd been making it. Instead of always looking for the "right" answers, now he's just looking for ways to experience God. And most often, he finds that it's all about loving the person God has placed near you.

Currently, Matt is a full-time pastor at a church near the Appalachian Trail. He still hikes when he can, and his church conference loves to host cookouts for the hikers on the trail so they can come down and enjoy good food and fellowship. Because loving others through the good, the bad, and the mundane is one of the greatest gifts of knowing Jesus.

- Think of one person God has put in your life you could reach out to with love, and do something kind for them today.
- Do you feel closer to people around you when you turn off your screens too?

Lamar Hardwick

Born 1978 • United States

Lamar Hardwick's voice was shaking when he told his congregation about his new diagnosis: Asperger's syndrome. Would they really want an autistic person leading their congregation? Would he be fired?

To his surprise, when Lamar announced his condition, they started clapping. Then one person stood. Then another. Before he knew it, Lamar was getting a standing ovation.

Growing up, Lamar had always felt different. People's facial expressions confused him—he couldn't understand what they meant. He didn't have many friends. He liked books better than people.

As a result, he did his best to develop ways to cope to help him get by in school. He learned that being smart wasn't cool, so even though he was bright, he stopped trying in his classes.

But after a near-fatal car wreck, Lamar turned his life around. He started trying again, and he started listening for what God might be calling him to do with his life. Ministry certainly wasn't the answer he expected to hear when he asked God for guidance. He thought it was a job for someone with people skills, but Lamar was faithful and listened.

After a lot of school and three different degrees, Lamar started working as an associate pastor at a church and was promoted to head pastor. But still, those challenges from childhood stayed with him and seemed to impact his job. So he went to see a therapist, and after a series of tests he got the news: his personality traits fell on the autism spectrum.

The love and support of his congregation wasn't the only good thing that came from Lamar's courage to go public as an adult with his autism diagnosis. Under Lamar's leadership, dozens of new families joined the church. Parents of children with special needs and adults with mental illness—basically anyone who felt *different*—found a home in Lamar's church.

Today, Lamar uses his platform as a pastor to raise awareness about autism and to encourage people on the spectrum to dream big and use their diagnosis to thrive.

- What's one thing that makes you different? What would it feel like to embrace that difference instead of hiding it?
- How did Lamar's vulnerability allow the people in his congregation to better love and accept him?

SCOTT Harrison

Born 1975 • United States

Scott Harrison lived a life most people would be jealous of. He partied a lot, slept all day, and got to schmooze with rich and beautiful people. He was making $5,000 a night to host parties at nightclubs.

Sounds fun, right? But after ten years of living the party life, Scott began to feel empty.

So he did the next most logical thing—at least in his mind. He applied to volunteer on a Christian-based hospital ship off the coast of Africa for a full year.

Talk about a turnaround!

It was his parents' idea. When the misery of his addiction-riddled party life became too much to handle, he'd asked for their advice. Almost overnight he went from being the most popular guy in the club to being a lowly volunteer. And it turned out to be the change that would save his life.

Over the course of his two years with the nonprofit Mercy Ships, Scott witnessed thousands of lives transformed—including his own. He saw doctors heal children born with cleft palates. He saw adults, once staggering under the weight of large tumors, set free. He saw blind people have their sight restored.

But Scott noticed something else as they sailed from city to city around Africa's coast. Most of the people Mercy Ships helped had no access to clean water.

Scott knew he could never return to his old life. He moved back to New York, but instead of visiting the clubs, he started using his connections to raise money for a new nonprofit, which he named charity: water.

Scott now leads a very different lifestyle. He has a wife and two children, and he spends his time helping people in poor parts of the world build wells. So far, charity: water has helped over 9.5 million people in twenty-seven countries get regular access to clean water. But Scott isn't stopping yet. A jaw-dropping 663 million people in the world still don't have clean water, and he doesn't plan to stop until he's reached all of them.

- Have you ever thought to thank God for the clean water your family has?
- Consider hosting a lemonade stand or bake sale to raise money for charity: water as a way to provide clean water to a family who doesn't have it.

Gary Haugen

Born 1963 • United States

Gary Haugen took a deep breath as his Harvard graduation ceremony ended. It was true—he was going to be a lawyer. It's what he'd worked so hard for, and now it was finally happening.

His first job had an interesting twist. When police officers weren't following the law, Gary was the guy who'd investigate. He found out he really enjoyed protecting innocent people from injustice.

Before long he was working with the US Department of Justice and the United Nations on human rights issues too. They asked him to take a trip that would change the course of his entire life. He was going to Rwanda, a country that had seen horrific warfare. Many innocent people had been killed. There, Gary faced evil head on. He instantly and forever decided to do his part to end it. Because for him, fighting injustice was part of his faith.

Jesus told his disciples, "The Spirit of the Lord is on me, because he has anointed me . . . to set the oppressed free" (Luke 4:18). Gary felt this same call, so when he got back home he used his legal expertise to form a new organization called International Justice Mission.

This team of lawyers, human rights workers, and undercover operatives plan secret missions inside some of the most dangerous parts of the world to rescue people who are in danger or oppressed. Once they've been rescued, he helps them put their lives back together again.

Right now, there are 25 million slaves around the world—people who are literally held against their will and forced to work without pay. For the record, that's more than there were at the time of the US Civil War. Gary is helping to rescue them, and because of him many people are living in freedom for the first time.

Turns out, you don't have to star in an action movie to take part in daring adventures and heroic rescues. You just need to be a man who listens to God's mission, opens his eyes to what's going on in the world, and is willing to get involved.

- What injustice in the world makes you angry?
- What issue would you like to write to your senators about, to ask them to take action?

THOMAS WADE JACKSON

Born 1967 • United States

When you are a Southern Baptist kid in Georgia, you're no stranger to potluck dinners full of pork BBQ, fried chicken, and biscuits with sausage gravy. It's not the background you'd expect a vegan to come from, but that's exactly how filmmaker Thomas Wade Jackson grew up.

As a child, Thomas loved Jesus's teachings about compassion. As an adult, he made compassion a priority. But the more he prayed, the more he worried he was only showing kindness to humans—not *all* of God's created beings. He decided then and there that he'd quit eating meat.

At lunch that day, he ordered his sandwich, "Vegetarian, please." The guy behind the counter clarified: "Vegetarian . . . or vegan?"

Thomas had never heard the word *vegan*, so he asked what it meant. "No animal products of any kind," the man answered. "No cheese, eggs, milk . . ."

"Vegan," Thomas answered.

From that day on, Thomas decided that the best choice for *him* was to eat a plant-only diet. What other people wanted to do with their diets was up to them. *Live and let live*, he thought.

But then his eyes were opened to the impact eating meat has on the environment—animals raised for food are the biggest reason for global warming, and not eating meat is an important thing we can do to protect the environment. Thomas asked God, "What do I do with this information?" God confirmed his gut feeling: Take a journey. Make a movie.

Thomas began to travel the world to make a documentary that challenges Christians to ask themselves, *What would it be like if I decided to stop eating meat?* He wants to share the good news: there's a better way.

God, in his love for us, created millions of varieties of plants—from big, juicy strawberries to crunchy, hearty chickpeas to the perfect bowl of popcorn to munch on while you watch a movie. These plants can nourish us, heal us, and give us active, healthy bodies to enjoy this amazing planet with. And that's what he wants kids today to know.

- Would your family be willing to try "meatless Mondays" once a week, to see if you might find a new family favorite dinner?
- Which is a bigger issue for you: eating healthier, not hurting animals, or helping the environment?

Lee Jong-rak

Born 1953 • South Korea

An alarm rings out, cutting through the air on an icy morning in the heart of Seoul, South Korea. Footsteps race toward the sound, but it's too late; the young mother is shuffling down the empty street, while her baby lies warm and safe in the drop box at Lee Jong-rak's church home.

When he was a child, Pastor Lee never dreamed he'd be running an orphanage one day. But he grew up watching his grandfather feed and care for his hungry neighbors. Compassion was in his blood and it was part of his faith.

Then Pastor Lee became a father to a child with a severe disability. His son was in the hospital for the better part of fourteen years. Through that experience, God showed Jong-rak his Word. Jong-rak has said his pain turned into thanksgiving, and he could now live a life that glorified God.

He did that by visiting the other patients at his son's hospital and praying with them for healing. One day a dying grandmother made a proposal: If Jong-rak would take care of her grandchild after she died, she would believe in Jesus.

Jong-rak was already overwhelmed with the tasks of caring for his own son, who couldn't talk or walk. But he desperately wanted this woman to know Jesus. So he agreed. Then, one night, another baby was left on his doorstep in a fishing tackle box. It was freezing, and she would have died if she had been found even moments later.

That was the beginning of Pastor Lee's new life as a father to many children. In 2009, he installed a warm, safe "drop box" at the gate to his home in Seoul. Parents who can't care for their children leave them there, and the babies are loved by Pastor Lee, his wife, and many volunteers. Over the years, more than 1,500 babies have been left in their care instead of being abandoned to die. Pastor Lee is dreaming of a society where there is no longer need for a baby box. But until then, he says, his job is to rescue and protect lives. That cannot be stopped, no matter what.

- Think about the people you see every day. Who could use some extra compassion in their lives?
- What can you do to help rescue and protect others?

Clarence Jordan

1912–1969 • United States

Clarence could smell the smoke before he reached the bombed-out market. The Ku Klux Klan had visited again. As Clarence approached the smoldering ruins of his roadside produce stand, he could see that this time, they had left nothing in their wake.

As scary as they were, the attacks were not a surprise. After all, Clarence was doing something completely radical—something that South Georgia in the 1950s wasn't quite ready for. He and another family had founded a small Christian farming community called Koinonia where black and white people worked, lived, and shared meals as equals. This was a crazy idea at the time.

You see, Clarence had finished seminary a few years before. He couldn't help but apply what he'd learned about Jesus's stereotype-busting, norm-shaking, life-rattling gospel to the problems in the South.

He couldn't stand seeing the black sharecroppers trapped in poverty by white landowners. He couldn't stand to hear black prisoners moaning in the night as they were tortured by white wardens. He couldn't stand the idea that white churches refused to welcome visitors with a darker skin tone.

So instead of accepting a well-paid job with a large Baptist church, Clarence helped create Koinonia, where he could live out his Christian ideals in a real way. Aside from the bombings, Koinonians survived other attacks from the community. Angry white neighbors shot at them, set their homes on fire, and boycotted their crops. But Clarence held steady and even kept his sense of humor about the situation. He started selling Koinonia's prize crop—pecans—through the mail with the slogan, "Help us ship the nuts out of Georgia."

Eventually Koinonia expanded to focus on providing quality homes to poor people in his community. Volunteers and new homeowners worked side by side to build simple, affordable housing with no-interest mortgages.

Unfortunately, Clarence died of a heart attack before he could live to see this new project become the nonprofit we know as Habitat for Humanity. Since its founding in 1976, Habitat has helped build almost a million homes around the world.

- Have you ever been mistreated for showing Jesus's love?
- Who in your community seems left out or not taken care of? Can you befriend them like Clarence did?

RUSSELL JEUNG

Born 1962 • United States

Murder Dubs" doesn't sound like the name of a very welcoming neighborhood. And it isn't. During the 1990s, this area of Oakland, California, was more likely to be mentioned on the evening news for drug deals gone wrong than for anything good. So it's strange that Russell Jeung and his wife would willingly move from their fancy San Francisco neighborhood to rent an apartment there. But that's exactly what they did in 1989.

The "why" may sound even weirder: Russell felt God was telling him to live in this cockroach-infested, inner-city apartment.

The thing is, this building was also full of Cambodian refugees. These were families who had moved to America to escape an evil tyrant back home. Although they were "safe" here in America, they were now living among the poverty, gangs, and drug-addicted people in one of California's poorest neighborhoods.

Russell's own grandparents immigrated to the United States and faced persecution because of their Asian heritage. Which is why he and his wife—and some friends of theirs—decided to help. They wanted to be all-in—not just visiting the neighborhood but actually living near these families in need.

First, they created an after-school safe space in their home the neighborhood kids could come to. These children got to experience what the love of Jesus looks like in a real, day-to-day way. Russell and his wife taught them to read, helped with homework, and kept them safe from the drug dealers trying to recruit them.

Russell could have been building his own career, but instead he was hanging posters of the ABCs on his apartment walls or filling out legal paperwork to take their abusive slumlord to court in order to get better living conditions for himself and his neighbors.

Before long, they became a thriving, joy-filled neighborhood known as the Oak Park Community. Here, Christians use their influence and power to help their neighbors who are new to this country. These immigrants are often suffering due to language barriers, culture shock, and post-traumatic stress. The support from Russell empowers his neighbors to make smart, positive decisions that will help them and their families live peacefully in their community.

- Can you think of a student at your school or church who you could help support?
- In what ways could you sacrifice your own comfort to help other people?

Martin Luther King Jr.

1929–1968 • United States

Martin Luther King Jr. sat on a cold, hard bench in a Birmingham city jail. Four days earlier, he'd been arrested for walking in a protest march without a permit. He was sore and bruised from the roughing up they gave him. His heart was heavy after reading the letter he was holding in his hand, written to him by a group of white pastors.

These pastors thought Martin was making great points about racism. Sure, they wrote, your people are being treated unfairly. These bombings and lynchings are bad. But, Reverend King, you just need to . . . chill out. Slow down. Let the courts handle it. It will work itself out in time.

Have you ever wanted something so badly you just couldn't wait for it, but you had to? Do you remember how frustrated that made you feel?

The black citizens of Birmingham, Selma, and the rest of the country didn't want to wait any longer. They were in danger now. They didn't have freedom now. And it was time for anyone who believed in Jesus to stand up against injustice . . . now.

Reverend King didn't want people to riot, though. He believed that nonviolent methods of protest—like marching with signs or sitting quietly at a segregated lunch counter—were the best way to bring about changes that would benefit not only the black community but all of America.

Not everyone agreed. While people marched for equal rights—like using the same bathrooms and water fountains or owning homes in the same neighborhoods—they were spat on, yelled at, and hit. Some even died.

Despite all these horrible things, Reverend King still had hope. He dreamed of a day when black kids and white kids could play together peacefully.

Eventually, even Martin Luther King Jr. gave his own life in the fight for Civil Rights. He was killed outside his hotel room in Memphis, Tennessee. But today, many of the dreams he spoke of have come true. And when you speak up against racism, you become part of that dream too.

- Have you witnessed racist comments or actions at your school or in your community?
- What is the right thing to say when someone makes a joke or comment that mocks another person because of their skin color, religion, or other feature?

PHIL KINGSTON

Born 1936 • Wales and England

Many years ago, if you asked Phil Kingston how he planned to spend his eighty-third birthday, he probably wouldn't have said getting arrested for climbing on top of a train to protest climate change. But Phil has witnessed a lot of changes to the environment in his more than eighty years on earth. Bad changes. He's seen carbon dioxide pollute fresh air. He's seen flooding and heat waves. He's seen a patch of trash the size of Texas in the ocean. This wasn't the earth he'd hoped to leave for his grandchildren.

Phil believes God created our beautiful earth, and he's willing to protest because he wants each of us to know what we can do to help save it. Scientists warn that global warming could raise ocean waters to dangerous levels—flooding cities near the beach. Farmers will have trouble growing our food, and some animals will die off . . . forever.

But the good news is, there are simple changes we can make to fix the problem. Phil climbs on top of trains or lays down in the middle of the road to block traffic so that people will hear his message that we need to use less plastic, eat less meat, conserve our water, and drive more energy-efficient cars. There are simple things even kids can do—like take shorter showers and play outside instead of using electricity for video games.

It might seem strange that a Christian would be willing to break the law, but Phil believes that unless we do dramatic things to bring attention to the problems in our environment, no one will make any changes. He says that it may be hard for younger people with jobs and families to be so willing to get in trouble with police, which is why the responsibility to protest falls on older adults like him. His career is over, so he has the freedom to risk arrest so that the message will get out. So far Phil has been arrested eleven times, and he doesn't plan on stopping until our planet is safe from harm.

- What's one small change you can make to use less energy?
- How can you use your role as a young person and student to advocate for a healthier planet?

Maximilian Kolbe

1894–1941 • Poland

Prisoner #16670 stepped forward. "I am a Catholic priest. Let me take his place." His fellow prisoner at the infamous Auschwitz prison camp, Franciszek Gajowniczek, gasped.

The commandant had just barked Franciszek's name, sentencing him to the starvation chamber. The words were out of his mouth before he realized he'd said them: "My wife! My children!" That's when the quiet priest stepped forward. The one who always stood last in the food line. The one who didn't sleep at night but came around to each man's bunk to offer his help. Franciszek couldn't believe it, and he held his breath as he waited for the commandant's answer.

Maximilian Kolbe, however, was completely at peace offering his own life for a stranger's. As a boy, he'd had a dream that changed his outlook on life. Mary, the mother of Jesus, asked him to choose between life as a priest or death as a martyr. Maximilian answered: "I accept them both."

That's why, when Nazi soldiers entered Poland, Maximilian didn't hesitate to hide Jewish refugees in his monastery. And he wasn't surprised when he was arrested and taken to Auschwitz in the cold winter of 1941.

Auschwitz was a terrible place. The guards were cruel and unforgiving. Prisoners were forced to work hard, long days of manual labor with almost no food. But the guards had one particularly terrifying rule: if one prisoner escapes, ten others will be killed in his place.

A prisoner from Maximilian's bunker vanished. The men were scared, but Maximilian chose bravery. It was likely the first and last time someone offered to die for another at Auschwitz.

Many years later, his guard confessed that the prisoners would all lie on the floor in utter weakness, but Father Kolbe was always kneeling or praying over the men. When he finally died, his face was radiant with joy.

Eventually, Franciszek Gajowniczek was able to return home. He told everyone about Father Kolbe's act of love, a shaft of light through the darkness of Auschwitz.

- What could you "sacrifice" for someone—such as doing your sibling's chores for them or helping your mom with the dishes instead of playing a video game?
- What's the bravest thing you've ever had to do?

JOHN LEWIS

Born 1940 • United States

When the policemen on horseback approached him on the Edmund Pettus Bridge in Selma, Alabama, John's heartbeat sped up. One officer emerged at the front of the pack, eased his horse forward, and ordered the march to stop.

John Lewis signaled the six hundred protestors behind him to halt. John and his co-leader Hosea Williams knew they were within their rights to be there, and they had an agenda. They were marching to draw national attention to the way black Alabamians were refused the right to vote.

Instead of leaving, Hosea calmly asked the major if they could have a word with him.

The major refused.

Hosea and John knew they were on thin ice. Every second they lingered on the bridge increased the risk of harm—for themselves and the rest of the marchers. As the silence stretched, they could hear each whinny of the horses, each scuffed hoof against the pavement.

Hosea took a deep breath and asked one more time.

The major still refused.

As the protestors looked at their leaders, John and Hosea did the only thing they knew to do. They knelt and offered a prayer.

In that moment, the major gave his troops the signal to attack. In a split second, the horses were plowing through the crowd as the policemen riding them bludgeoned protestors and sprayed tear gas into their eyes.

John suffered a skull fracture, and he and sixteen other protestors went to the hospital. Dozens more were injured, but not before speaking to reporters about the need for equality in Alabama.

Luckily, the massacre had been caught on film. It would bring the publicity the Civil Rights movement desperately needed. After several more protests, including another Selma march led by Martin Luther King Jr. himself, President Lyndon Johnson passed the Voting Rights Act of 1965 that protected black Americans from discrimination when exercising their right to vote.

Today, John Lewis serves in the United States House of Representatives, where he continues to work toward the fulfillment of Dr. King's dream of equal rights for all people.

- How can you peacefully stand up for equality for all people?
- What injustices do you see in your own community today?

Eric Liddell

1902–1945 • Scotland and China

Eric Liddell stepped off the train in rural, war-torn China. This would be his home—again—now that he was starting missions work as a teacher. And as he glanced around the campus that would be his new high school and saw the children running and playing, his mind flashed back to the summer of 1924 in Paris, France.

Everyone had expected Eric to win the gold medal in the 100-meter race, but he chose not to run so he could honor the Sabbath with a day of complete rest. Even though it wasn't his best event, he entered the 400-meter race and won first place, even setting a new world record. But now in China, the country where he was born as a child of missionaries, he'd show his love for sport by serving as a referee on the playing fields for Chinese kids. He wanted them to be carefree, even though Japanese soldiers were about to invade their homes.

When the British authorities warned that all citizens should leave China immediately, Eric stayed to continue his work. Soon, he was arrested and placed in a Japanese internment camp.

Eric's always-positive attitude continued, even in these harsh circumstances. He taught science to the children so they wouldn't fall behind in school. He helped the older people in camp, making sure they had the supplies they needed. Even though he was tired at night, he could still be found staying up late, organizing events like chess matches, square dances, or soccer games to keep spirits up.

Eventually, Eric's health gave out. He died in the internment camp just five months before it was freed. He had been a man overflowing with good humor, one friend said, and it spilled over to everyone around him. Even though he is still the most famous Scottish athlete, Eric Liddell was buried on a tiny plot behind the Japanese officer's quarters marked by a small wooden cross.

In life, Eric had never sought glory for himself but only for God. His death was no different.

- What does a Sabbath day of rest look like for your family? Should you consider making any changes to your routines?
- What practical things you can do to stay positive when parts of your life are miserable?

Janani Luwum

1922–1977 • Uganda

Even though Janani Luwum knew his job would not be easy, he was honored to be appointed the new archbishop of Uganda and three surrounding countries. Only a few years earlier, the government of Uganda had been overthrown and taken over by Idi Amin, the army chief of staff. Since then, Ugandans had been living under a strict military dictatorship.

Amin was a jealous leader and had anyone who disagreed with him killed. He wanted everyone of Asian heritage removed from the country, and he ordered many Christians killed for even small offenses. One pastor who read a psalm over the radio was put to death just because the psalm mentioned Israel.

Archbishop Luwum, however, was known for being a shepherd to his people and for loving young people. He couldn't bear to see his church members persecuted in this way. So he joined with Roman Catholic and Muslim leaders to confront Amin about his cruelty and use of violence.

Unfortunately, it changed nothing.

Shortly after, a small group of rebels tried to win back power from Amin, but they were quickly defeated by his troops. Even though it was a small insurrection, it stoked the flames of Amin's paranoia. He decided then that he would kill anyone he even remotely suspected of treason. In a fit of jealousy, he killed thousands of innocent people, including everyone in the former president's hometown.

Janani Luwum and his fellow priests decided to protest again. But this time, Amin didn't react so kindly. He accused Janani of treason. He even staged a public trial where he falsely convicted the men of smuggling arms and supporting the ousted president. Amin allowed the other clerics to leave, but he kept Janani.

The last thing Janani said before the others left was, "They are going to kill me. I am not afraid." And he was right.

Janani is celebrated as a modern martyr. Even today his courage inspires others to follow Christ by standing up to injustices when they see them happen.

- Have you ever felt jealous? What's a good way to deal with that feeling?
- Have you ever had to stand up to someone because you knew what they were doing was wrong?

PAUL MBITHI

Born 1960 • Kenya

For nineteen years, Paul Mbithi worked for KLM Airlines in Nairobi. Every day as Paul passed the slums on his way to work in his neatly pressed suit, something didn't sit right with him. He'd see toddlers sitting all alone on trash heaps. Children slept beside puddles of sewage and wore nothing but soiled rags.

Paul thought that maybe God was calling him to something more than financial stability and a good career. As a result, he decided to join the ministry team of the local church he'd been attending. For ten years, he worked under a head pastor, learning and serving, until one day he shared his desire to start an orphanage to shelter the children he saw in the slums.

But the head pastor said no. He only wanted to focus on preaching and spreading the Word of God itself.

Paul was discouraged, but he kept thinking about Jesus. Jesus never let his crowds go hungry while he preached. He fed the hungry *and* shared the gospel.

So Paul struck out on his own.

Paul started his own church, and he and his wife, Grace, kept an eye out for homeless children nearby. Eventually Grace noticed that the same four young boys kept showing up at their local outdoor market. Each day they hid until the shopkeepers left and then scavenged for spare beans and corn. One day Grace approached and asked them to come to Sunday school.

Paul and Grace took the small boys in, and eventually the boys spread the word to other homeless children they knew. Before Paul and Grace knew it, the orphanage had grown to almost one hundred children.

Since then, the orphanage has burned down twice—fires are just one hazard of living in the slums. Despite the risks, Paul and Grace refuse to rebuild somewhere safer. They prefer to live where the homeless children can find them, right in the heart of the need.

- What needs do you see in your own community? How can you help?
- How do you treat kids who are different from you?

Aristides de Sousa Mendes

1885–1954 • Portugal

Aristides de Sousa Mendes lay in his bed, agonizing over his decision. He knew that if he issued visas for the Jews, against the orders of the Portuguese prime minister, he and his whole family would be punished. His glamorous life as a diplomat would be over.

But Aristides also knew that if he did nothing, the Jews trying to escape Germany could be sent to concentration camps—or killed before they even got there.

As he tossed and turned, Aristides remembered the Polish rabbi he'd met at the Bordeaux consulate among the other Jewish refugees. The rabbi was fleeing persecution with his family, but when Aristides offered him a visa, he refused. The rabbi didn't want a free pass out of the country until all the Jews waiting at the consulate had one.

The rabbi's courage inspired Aristides, and on the third day he rose from his bed and declared that everyone was getting a visa, no matter their race or religion. He decided that he would rather betray the prime minister than betray his Christian faith.

With the help of the rabbi and his assistant, Aristides set up an assembly line for signing visas. When his hand got too tired to sign his entire name, he simply wrote "Mendes." Aristides signed tens of thousands of visas over the next few days. Eventually, the Portuguese prime minister found out about his rescue efforts and ordered that the consulate be shut down.

Unfortunately, when Aristides returned to Portugal, his career was over. The prime minister stripped him of his job and made sure he never worked again. He and his family only survived because a local Jewish soup kitchen fed them when they ran out of food. For a man born into wealth and social status, Aristides ended his life in poverty and obscurity.

Thankfully, Aristides's children have worked hard to restore his reputation since his death and to shine a light on his heroic efforts. There's even a database for people who received visas signed by Aristides. They and their family members number in the tens of thousands and live across the globe. Many are alive today simply because of Aristides's sacrificial work.

- Have you ever been punished for doing something good?
- How do you make tough decisions?

MICHELANGELO

1475–1564 • Italy

When Michelangelo heard that the pope was commissioning him to paint the ceiling of the Sistine Chapel, he was a little confused. After all, Michelangelo was a *sculptor*—and a brilliant one at that. He didn't have much painting experience. Michelangelo didn't know it at the time, but a fellow artist named Bramante had encouraged the pope to pick Michelangelo for just that reason. He was jealous of Michelangelo's success and hoped he would fail miserably—and publicly—at painting the famous church.

But, boy, did Bramante's challenge backfire. If there was a choice between going big or going home, Michelangelo definitely went big. He decided to paint a series of fresco panels that would tell the story of the Bible, from Adam and Eve's big mistake in the garden of Eden to the prophets to the ancestors of Jesus.

Many days, while painting his epic images of God's story, Michelangelo wondered about his own faith. He'd always felt that God demanded perfection from him, but he knew he could never live up to that. Neither could his paintings. In fact, he even had to start over on the Sistine Chapel ceiling once because the paintings started to mold.

Ultimately, it took him four years to finish this project, and the Sistine Chapel was transformed. But Michelangelo was transformed on the inside too. He'd come to realize that faith alone connected people to God—not their good works or impressive talent. He began to view art as a way to investigate and reflect on God, and he hoped other people would use his art to do the same.

People today still travel from around the world to see the Sistine Chapel ceiling in person, and its beauty and biblical storytelling still inspire wonder and awe. Proof that God can use anything—even a little jealousy—to draw people to him.

- How can you take something negative and use it to show God's glory?
- What piece of art inspires you?

enrique morones

Born 1956 • United States

Dust kicked up behind the caravan of cars heading into the California desert. The temperature was well over 100 degrees, and the sun was beating down on the small team of volunteers led by Enrique Morones. They were miles from home, in the middle of nowhere, dropping rations of water for migrant families who would be passing through this barren landscape soon. For those travelers, the water stations could be the difference between life and death.

As a proud American *and* a proud Mexican, Enrique knows firsthand how dangerous the journey can be. Deciding to cross the desert—full of coyotes, extreme heat, and dangerous men—is no easy task, but for many families it is their only hope to escape the drug lords and corrupt governments back home. Though after walking miles in the blistering sun, many collapse from lack of water.

In 1986, Enrique knew he had to do something to help, and the words of Jesus played in his mind: "For I was hungry and you gave me something to eat, I was thirsty and you gave me something to drink" (Matthew 25:35). Providing water and food, which are necessary to stay alive, was the first thing he did. But he didn't stop there. Enrique's ministry, Border Angels, helps immigrant families once they reach his hometown of San Diego as well. They help them understand their rights, and teach them how to immigrate legally. Meeting Enrique and his team when they first arrive in America is the warm welcome these immigrants hope for.

Even though to Enrique it seems like common sense to help people who are hurting, others don't always agree with his mission. In fact, some volunteers are even arrested for simply helping an immigrant who is hurt or sick. But Enrique will continue to help, he'll continue to take water, he'll continue to advocate for immigrants, and he'll continue to tell their stories. He hopes that if people understand what immigration is really like, they'll have a little more compassion, love, and understanding too.

- If you know someone who was born in another country, ask them what their experience coming to America was like.
- What can you do to help someone who is suffering in your neighborhood or community?

DIKEMBE MUTOMBO

Born 1966 • Democratic Republic of the Congo

The sun was hot as Dikembe Mutombo walked through the bustling Central Market in the Democratic Republic of Congo. He was dreaming of going to America, where he would watch the Globetrotters play basketball and might even meet an astronaut.

But his thoughts were interrupted by shouts from local boys: "Giraffe!" they laughed. "Monster!"

Dikembe ran home, humiliated once again by the neighborhood bullies. It was hard enough living in one of the poorest and most violent countries in the world, but standing out because you're really, really tall didn't make it any easier.

Luckily, Dikembe had kind parents who loved him and loved Jesus. They reminded him that being teased for his height was nothing compared to the kids around him suffering from measles and malaria.

So Dikembe decided to fight back . . . by helping. He studied to become a doctor and enrolled at Georgetown University on an academic scholarship. During his sophomore year, the school's basketball coach asked the 7'2" student to try out for the basketball team.

Turns out, Dikembe was really good at basketball. In fact, he was playing in the NBA before he knew it. They called him Mt. Mutombo, one of the greatest shot blockers of all time. But as much as the crowds loved him in America, he was an even bigger hero back home.

Between seasons, Dikembe went home to visit his family and to help his hurting country. He visited refugees. He paid for the women's basketball team to play in the Olympics. He got married and adopted four kids—all while he was still playing basketball in the NBA.

But Dikembe's greatest accomplishment isn't on the court—it's the Biamba Marie Mutombo hospital he built, with millions of his own dollars, in honor of his mom. There, hundreds of thousands of Congolese people get state-of-the-art medical care.

He says the hospital was a place people went to die when he was growing up. Now, it's a place they go to recover . . . and live.

- What can you do to be part of a solution to a problem the world is facing?
- Do you think it's more exciting to be famous or to help other people?

THE NAGASAKI MARTYRS

1597 • Japan

From the deck of the large European ship, Father Francis Xavier could see waves lapping at the shore of Kyushu Island, Japan. As they veered toward the port ahead, he wondered what he was getting into. Japan was a mysterious land, known for its beautiful art and civilized tea ceremonies, but also for its terrifying shogun military leaders and brutal feudal lords known as *daimyōs*. It was here, at the edge of the world, that he hoped to spread the good news of Jesus's love.

In the beginning, they found support from the local shogun and daimyō. Soon a small but strong group of Christians was thriving in Kagoshima. But eventually it became clear the government only hoped the missionaries would help them start trade with Europe, and when that didn't happen tensions began to run high. Before long, any "foreign" influence in Japan was seen as a threat, and all foreign influence in Japan was completely banned. That meant all Christians would have to abandon their faith . . . or be killed.

Six missionaries and twenty Japanese Christians—including three young boys—refused to give up on Jesus, so the shogun had them imprisoned until their execution. But before he killed them, he decided to march them in chains through the snow to Nagasaki so the growing Christian community there would see their executions and give up their faith. But it didn't work—the people continued to worship Jesus. Thirty-five years later, another fifty-five Christians were killed. After their deaths, Christianity was officially outlawed in Japan.

But here's the thing: outlawing Jesus *still* didn't work. All of the remaining Christians went "underground" with their faith, meaning they worshiped in secret so no one would know. Even though the shoguns came up with crazy ways to try to draw them out—like asking them to stomp all over a picture of Jesus to prove they didn't love him—it didn't work. And when missionaries were finally allowed back in Japan two hundred and fifty years later, they found a community of hidden Christians that had survived all those years.

- Have you ever felt like you needed to hide your faith?
- Have you ever gone somewhere new, exciting, and a little scary, and let people there know you're a Christian?

Paul Niehaus and Michael Faye

Born 1982 • United States, Africa

As students in economics (the science of how people make, spend, and transfer money) at Harvard, Paul Niehaus and Michael Faye were picky about who they gave their money to. It wasn't that they didn't want to give. The two young men were Christians and believed in giving to the church regularly. It was just that, as academics, they also believed in research-based evidence.

One day they had a new idea: What if they gave money directly to poor people and trusted them to make wise decisions with it?

It was a bold idea, but they decided to give it a shot.

Around this time, SIM cards in cell phones were allowing people to send money to even the most remote regions of Africa and Asia. Paul and Michael used the new technology to start a charity called GiveDirectly.

Their nonprofit does what the name says. It allows donors to give cash to the neediest people in developing countries, then lets the recipients make decisions about how to use it.

Michael and Paul were eager to see how this new, easier form of aid would succeed.

The results? Sending cash directly to extremely poor people led to great long-term results.

One man, who had been trained as a welder but couldn't afford welding equipment, used his money to buy tools and open his own shop. Another family used theirs to buy goats so they could produce milk for their family. They also started breeding goats to sell. Others simply used their money to make sure their children could eat and go to school.

Paul and Michael's research showed that people who received a cash boost were earning 40 to 80 percent more money five years later.

Today, GiveDirectly is ranked as one of the most effective charities in the world. Since it started in 2009, they've given away tens of millions of dollars—all directly into the hands of people who need it most.

- How can you help people in need around you while still respecting them?
- Have you ever used outside-the-box thinking to solve a problem? How can you apply this type of thinking to challenges in your life?

ROBBY NOVAK

Born 2004 • United States

Annnnd, action!"

Robby Novak smiled for the camera in his suit and tie. To the viewers, it would look like he was sitting in the White House Oval Office (well, *almost*). Robby was actually at home in front of a big piece of butcher paper with the presidential seal drawn on it. His brother-in-law, Brad, was behind the camera . . . and it was time for another pep talk video.

Robby's life hasn't always been easy, but his faith has helped him keep a positive outlook. When he was a little kid, he and his sister were adopted from the foster care system. He has a rare disease called osteogenesis imperfecta—those are really big words that mean his bones break easily. In fact, they've broken more than seventy times.

It would be easy for him to complain about that, but he wants people to see the joy God gives him instead of his casts and surgery scars. Which is why he and his brother-in-law started making funny, inspiring videos from "Kid President." (That's Robby, in case you haven't figured it out yet.)

Social media can be a tough place for kids, where people feel bullied more than loved. But Robby's idea is to make the world as good a place as he can, while he can. How does he do that? Robby suggests we treat everybody like it's their birthday, every single day. Be *that* nice to the people around you.

As it turns out, lots of people think that's a great idea. Even though his videos started as fun messages to family and friends, he's now become famous for them. His "Pep Talk from Kid President" video on YouTube has been watched more than 44 million times. Whoa! And Kid President even got to meet the real President Obama once.

Just goes to show you, being the nice guy really does get you places in life. And the world sure could use even more of Kid President's positivity.

- What's one difficult thing in your life you could choose to have a great attitude about?
- What does it mean to "treat everyone like it's their birthday, every day"?

JOHN G. PATON

1824–1907 • Scotland and the New Hebrides Islands

The sun was rising over the hills on a beautiful Scottish morning. Twelve-year-old John Paton could hear the sheep bleating in the distance as he headed out the door of his family's cottage to do his chores. His father was already awake and in his prayer closet. One day, John hoped to have the same devotion to God that his father did.

As a kid, John dreamed about going overseas to tell other people about Jesus. But he worked fourteen hours a day for his father, with just two hours for meals. And evening time was often spent studying, not eating. In case you can't tell, John was a very hard worker.

Finally, the day came when John was old enough to fulfill his dream. He walked down the country lane with his father, where they hugged and said their final goodbyes. John walked another forty miles to the town of Kilmarnock, then took a train to Glasgow. After he finished his training there, he boarded a ship for the New Hebrides Islands in the South Pacific. The first missionaries to step ashore there had been killed—and eaten by the local cannibals—within minutes of their arrival.

John was more fortunate than some who went before him, but living among this superstitious group was quite the culture shock. Still, he respected the local people and wanted to help them. A horrible practice called blackbirding, where the locals were kidnapped at night and sold as slaves, was spreading fear. John dedicated himself to stopping it once and for all.

First, he learned to speak to the locals and put their language into a written form. He translated the Bible so they could read it in their own words. He and his wife taught them to read, sew, and make hats so they had money. And he set up medical clinics to help the sick.

John gave up everything he knew and loved, including his dear father, to improve the lives of people he had never met. And he wrote in his autobiography that finally worshiping Jesus with those strangers was the greatest happiness he'd ever known.

- Does the idea of traveling across the world scare you or excite you?
- Do you think you're a hard worker like John?

COLIN POWELL

Born 1937 • United States

We're going down! We're going down!"

Colin Powell, a major in the US army, was traveling by helicopter through Vietnam while the country waged war on the ground beneath him. His chopper was going down, and everyone's life was in danger.

When they hit, Powell was alive and, miraculously, not critically injured. Once he realized he was okay, he got up . . . and ran straight back into the burning wreckage. Eventually, he saved every passenger from the helicopter, even though he had to pull burning metal away with his bare hands.

That's just one reason most people use the word *kind* when they talk about the former Secretary of State General Colin Powell.

Kindness has always been in Colin Powell's blood. As a young Jamaican American growing up in the South Bronx, Colin attended a Christian church but many of his neighbors were Jewish. Instead of taking an us-versus-them attitude, he decided to learn Yiddish so he could talk to them in their language. He even came to their houses and helped them with tasks they weren't allowed to do on the Sabbath, a job called the *Shabbos goy*.

Eventually, Colin left his neighborhood and joined the military. He served on two missions during the Vietnam War and eventually became an advisor to many presidents.

They called him "the reluctant warrior" because his first instinct was always to look for non-military solutions to international crises. And when he did have to involve his soldiers in a conflict, he always designed a plan that would be most likely to win with the least casualties.

But Colin says he learned the real meaning of kindness at his Episcopal church when a visiting priest gave a sermon that really impacted him. The priest said that kindness isn't about being nice. It's about recognizing that another person deserves care and respect.

Now, whether Colin is supporting women's causes or helping to mentor at-risk kids in America, he chooses to love others with the same care and respect for all human life Jesus did.

- What's one kind thing you can do today?
- How do you choose to be kind to your "enemies"?

CHARLES ROBINSON

Born 1966 • Choctaw Nation of Oklahoma

Stepping through the woods silently, the young Choctaw boy kept his eyes focused on the rabbit just a few feet away. If he could get closer, he'd bring home a delicious dinner for his family that night. But just as he drew an arrow from his quiver, voices in the distance startled the bunny away.

The boy was startled too. The voices were too loud, and the words strange. He kept himself hidden as he peered through the trees. Little did he know, the Spanish explorers he saw were going to bring an end to the way his people lived forever.

Fast forward six hundred years, and Charles Robinson's mission is to right the wrongs of the past . . . as a way of showing Jesus's love for Native people like himself.

His first step is educating children about the beautiful, vibrant traditions of Native people. Ever since Charles was introduced to a classroom of students as a "real, live Indian," he knew there were some serious misunderstandings he wanted to correct. So he and his family wear their beautiful handmade ceremonial clothes, perform dances, and demonstrate how to use traditional Choctaw tools. And he teaches students how to value and respect Native cultures.

But that's not all Charles does. See, many of the bad things that happened to America's first people over the years were done by people who called themselves Christians. Native nations lost their land, their rights, and so much more. Even though many of the Native people Charles visits believe in an all-knowing, all-powerful God and even accept Jesus . . . they're wary of "Christians."

Charles teaches that all of creation, including the beautiful traditions of Native people, are valued by God. He helps the tribes preserve their original languages and teach them to their children. He puts together support groups for victims of violence. He delivers baskets of essential supplies to struggling families. And he argues for better representation for Native people in Washington, D.C.

All of this is his way of loving Native people as Jesus would.

- Do you know which Native nation claims the land where you currently live?
- What's one thing you can do to honor the cultures of America's original people?

óscar Romero

1917–1980 • El Salvador

As Archbishop Óscar Romero read the lines of his weekly message on the radio, he felt his hands begin to shake. He shuffled his notes and took a breath. He knew that his next statement could change his life forever.

Saying a quick prayer to God, Óscar forged onward to his boldest paragraph. "Brothers," he said, speaking to the soldiers in El Salvador's army, "you belong to our own people. You kill your own brothers . . . [but] the law of God that says 'Do not kill!' should prevail."

He felt a bead of sweat trickle down his forehead. He kept going.

"In the name of God, cease the repression!"

Óscar knew he'd put his life in grave danger, but it was his only option. Not even a year ago, a military dictatorship had risen to power, and troops were slaughtering innocent, poor El Salvadorans. Priests and nuns had been attacked, and churches had been raided. On top of that, the military had taken control of all news outlets in the country so journalists couldn't report what was really happening.

So Óscar began broadcasting his weekly sermon without the government's permission. Each week, he'd preach the gospel *and* give the real stories of the people whom the president had ordered to be murdered, tortured, or kidnapped that week. Soon Óscar was the only source of real news in the country.

The day after Óscar issued his bold challenge, he was performing mass in a small hospital chapel. A red car pulled up on the street outside, and a man with a gun quickly stepped to the chapel doors. Oscar was shot and died instantly, but his murder and public funeral finally shined a spotlight on the wrongs happening in El Salvador.

Today, Óscar is beloved throughout Latin America for standing up to protect the people. He's even officially been made a saint in the Catholic church.

- Can you think of anyone you know who is "voiceless"? How can you help?
- Have you ever come across censorship (someone telling you what you can and cannot say in public) before? How can you continue to speak truth?

Fred Rogers

1928–2003 • United States

Fred Rogers sat cross-legged on his bedroom floor. It was a hot, muggy day outside in his Pennsylvania town, and his mother had forbidden Fred from going outside to play because the weather might bring on an asthma attack. But that was okay. Fred was laughing and playing pretend with two of his very best friends.

There was only one thing a little different about Fred's friends: they were imaginary!

In addition to his asthma, Fred's shy personality and embarrassment about his weight made it difficult for him to make real-life friends at his school. Instead, he stayed in his room and imagined worlds full of characters he'd created himself.

Still, Fred was lonely. People were always telling him that his sensitivity and introversion were bad—something he should hide—so he kept to himself.

But one person told him differently. Fred's grandfather, Mr. McFeely, encouraged Fred to be himself.

As Fred grew older and got more confident, he began to think that maybe his grandad was right. Maybe his unique personality traits were strengths, not weaknesses. Maybe he could use these gifts to help other children who felt alone.

So after graduating from seminary, Fred decided to start a television program to help kids understand real compassion and kindness, the kind Jesus taught. On his show, Mr. Rogers told children what his grandfather had told him: they were special just the way they were. Mr. Rogers never talked down to children. When Sen. Robert Kennedy was killed, Mr. Rogers gently explained what *assassination* meant and helped children process their feelings. In a time when people with disabilities were misunderstood, Mr. Rogers invited a boy in an electric wheelchair onto the show to chat. When many swimming pools in the US were only for white people or black people, never both, Mr. Rogers and his African American mailman splashed their feet in a backyard pool together. All this, *and* he got to talk with Henrietta Pussycat, X the Owl, and Daniel Tiger every day!

Mr. Rogers' Neighborhood became one of the longest-running and most-beloved children's shows in television history.

- What are some of the unique traits that make you special?
- How can you use your imagination to get through a difficult time?

James Shaw Jr.

Born 1988 • United States

James Shaw Jr. was enjoying a late-night meal at Waffle House when he heard a loud *boom* and saw the glass across from him shatter and fall. James looked up just in time to see a shooter entering the restaurant. They locked eyes. A half second later, the shooter raised his machine gun and started firing at random. Customers and cooks ducked while others fell to the ground.

James and his friend ran into the hallway toward the bathroom to protect themselves. From there, they urged the other patrons who were hiding to stay quiet and calm.

But James knew that sooner or later the armed man would find them in their hiding spot and they'd have to fight back.

As James looked on, the shooter paused to look down at his gun. In this moment, James said he heard his father saying, "Always be smarter than the thing you're working on." James was an electrician and had usually applied this idea to complicated electrical wiring problems, not active shooter scenarios. But maybe that saying could help him here too? He was scared, but he could feel that God was with him.

In a split second, James decided to tackle the shooter while he was distracted. James ran up from behind and grabbed the gun barrel with both hands. He severely burned his hands but managed to seize the AR-15 from the shooter and toss it over the counter, out of reach.

And with that, the rest of the patrons were safe.

James says he's just a regular person, not a hero. In fact, that morning after the attack, he went to church like it was any other day. He thinks people should focus on the victims of the Waffle House shooting, not on his bravery. In fact, James has raised almost a quarter of a million dollars for the families of the victims, and he says he's even considering running for mayor of Nashville to help find solutions for other issues in the city.

Whatever the thirty-one-year-old ends up doing next, Nashvillians know James has their backs.

- How can you "be smarter than the thing you're working on"?
- What does true heroism mean to you?

Bryan Stevenson

Born 1959 • United States

As Bryan Stevenson walked up to his new classroom on the first day of school, he took a deep breath and adjusted the straps of his backpack. In first grade, he'd gone to a "colored" school that was just for black children, but this year his school had been desegregated. That meant that black and white kids would go to school together now.

But Bryan quickly realized that even though his school was *legally* desegregated, there was still a divide between the different races. Kind of like the way black people could go to the white dentist, but they had to use the back door. Or how he and his mom had to wait hours for his polio vaccination so all the white kids could get theirs first.

That never sat right with Bryan, who was born with a gut-level sense of right and wrong. After all, his grandmother had been the daughter of slaves, and she'd taught him about injustice early on. And didn't his beloved Bible say that *all* men are created equal?

So when Bryan graduated from Harvard Law School, he started working for an organization that provides legal help to people on death row. And he quickly realized that many, many of the people who were sentenced to death, or to life in prison, were black. This, too, rubbed Bryan the wrong way. He knew from his childhood that there was still plenty of racism happening today. What if some of these men were innocent but had been convicted because of their race? What if they didn't get fair trials because they were poor or came from bad neighborhoods?

As a result, Bryan started the Equal Justice Initiative, an organization that helps fight for quality legal representation for everyone—no matter where they came from or the color of their skin. Bryan believes that as Christians, it's our job to be the hope in hopeless places, and to extend mercy wherever we can.

- Do you see any unofficial segregation in your own school? How can you work to change it?
- What does mercy mean to you?

J. R. R. TOLKIEN

1892–1973 • England

J. R. R. Tolkien set down his papers, picked up his glass, and took a slow sip from his drink as he waited to hear what his mates—a group known as the Inklings—would think of his newest story.

He thought back to his aunt Jane's farm called Bag End and his holiday hiking in Switzerland, both of which inspired this quirky tale about hobbits, adventure, grave danger, and, of course, faith.

Faith was a topic that came up often between these men. In fact, in his deep discussions late at night, his friend C. S. Lewis had started showing signs he was loosening his tight grip on his atheist beliefs and might open his heart to the love of God.

He understood Lewis's resistance to God. Tolkien's life had been hard too—orphaned by age twelve, raised by a Catholic priest who he considered a father but who nearly ruined his relationship with the woman he loved, and . . . of course, the war. The horrible war.

But ultimately his love of words had led him to a job writing for the Oxford English Dictionary, then as a professor at Leeds and eventually at Oxford University, where he met Lewis.

Tolkien rode his bike to the pub every week to meet with the Inklings. They'd take turns sharing their writing ideas and getting constructive criticism from each other. But Lewis had been asking more and more about Tolkien's devout Roman Catholic faith, and Tolkien was hopeful his friend would come to love Jesus too.

In the end, of course, Lewis did come to love Jesus, and his Chronicles of Narnia books are beloved by kids around the world as much as Tolkien's the Lord of the Rings series and *The Hobbit* are. Tolkien's wish was that his readers would be inspired by his stories and explore their own imaginations. For decades, his books have helped them do that.

- What's your favorite book? Did it help you understand God better?
- Who could you share God's love with? And how do you imagine they might change the world because of it?

DESMOND TUTU

Born 1931 • South Africa

Desmond!" Bishop Nkoane shouted over the crowd. "You must come *now!*"

The short 5'3" Anglican bishop and Nobel Peace Prize winner pushed his way through the angry mob. He could see the car on fire up ahead, and the enraged crowd was pouring gasoline onto a man nearby. The suspected informer would be dead in seconds if Desmond didn't get there soon.

Bishop Desmond Tutu did get there in time, and he managed to convince the men that killing this black man, who they suspected of spying on them for the white police force, would only hurt their cause, not help it. In a country that was so racially divided, they must stick together to win the freedoms they longed for.

Desmond Tutu loved this land. He'd been born in South Africa, raised in a poor part of town in a mud-brick building on the grounds of the school where his father worked. He loved heroes in comic books and fairy tales—a longing for justice ran deep in him.

When he became older, he left to study at King's College in England. He learned a lot while he was there, but the experience of living in a non-apartheid country (where whites and blacks lived together as equals) changed him forever.

When he returned home to preach, he joined protests and called for equal rights for all people. When others didn't speak up, he called their silence "deafening." He encouraged nonviolent protest and asked foreign countries to make it harder for South Africa to do business until their black citizens had rights too.

He met with foreign leader after leader after leader . . . with no results. When people asked him why he didn't give up, he mentioned Moses. What if Moses had quit going back to Pharaoh to ask for the Israelites' freedom?

Eventually, Tutu's dream to live in a "Rainbow Nation"—where God's people of every color lived as equals—came true. Black leaders who'd been in prison were released, and South Africa even had a black president. And even though life in South Africa isn't perfect, his faith in God's justice became reality.

- Just like Desmond Tutu identified with Moses, what Bible character do you most identify with?
- Even though you're small now, how can you help protect others around you?

we carry kevan team:

kevan chandler, tom troyer, philip keller, benjamin duvall, danny tenney, and luke thompson

Embarked 2016 • Worldwide

A lifelong lover of C. S. Lewis and G. K. Chesterton, Kevan Chandler had always wanted to experience the rolling hills and bustling streets of England. Not to mention the rest of Europe. But for Kevan, who has spinal muscular atrophy, just getting around his hometown was a struggle. Every excursion involved strategic plans centered around wheelchair ramps, elevators, and vans with electric lifts. He didn't think he could ever take a gap year or travel Europe like other people his age.

But then Kevan and his friends had an idea. What if they could design a backpack for Kevan that allowed them to carry him around? That way, he would be able to go places that weren't wheelchair accessible. The Bible had always taught them that loving their neighbors could change the world, and maybe this was their chance.

So Kevan and his friends bought a toddler backpack and adjusted it to fit Kevan's bigger— but not much bigger—body. Then, with the help of many donors, they took off on their adventure.

He'd previously only been to disability-accessible areas, but Kevan could now go anywhere. His friends hiked with him up a craggy mountain peak on a remote Irish island and danced with him in the cobbled streets of Paris—places he never dreamed he could have gone before.

Kevan and his friends made a documentary about their trip so they could show the world how their understanding of Jesus's love had given them a new way to think about accessibility and loving their friend. Maybe accessibility wasn't just about ramps and chairs. Maybe it was also about community, creativity, and love. And it turned out that many people needed to hear their message.

So Kevan and his friends decided to visit China, a place where many people with disabilities were treated like outsiders. They wanted to show everyone that disabilities didn't have to be so limiting. They visited orphanages for disabled children and brought several of their specially designed backpacks for the children to use.

Together, they spread hope and imagination, helping kids with disabilities to dream big.

- How can you help a friend overcome a limitation?
- Have you ever used your imagination to solve a tough problem?

WILLIAM WILBERFORCE

1759–1833 • England

William Wilberforce shuffled down the London alleyway, squinting to see where he was going in the evening dusk. His eyesight had been poor since he was a child. As he turned a corner, a man jumped out and bludgeoned William over the head. William fell to the ground, dizzy, but he could guess who this man was: someone whose livelihood depended on the slave trade William was trying to abolish.

William hadn't always been a crusader for justice. In fact, as a young man he'd been a heavy drinker and gambler, usually the last to leave the party and the most likely to skip class.

Then, as a young adult who'd recently been elected to British parliament—thanks to his family's money—one of William's friends told him about Jesus. William, a highly intellectual graduate of Cambridge University, balked at the idea at first. How could he believe in such irrational things? But over time, as he read the Bible, William became convicted of his sinful nature and gave his life to God.

It turns out that God had great plans for him! God called William to abolish the slave trade in Britain. It was a grizzly business. British ships sailed to Africa and captured people there, chaining them up in ships and transporting them to Europe and America to be sold as slaves. The more William learned about it, the more appalled he was. So he devoted the rest of his life to ending the practice.

The problem was, the slave trade made many people in Britain very, very wealthy. They weren't going to give up without a fight. William suffered many defeats in Parliament and was even beaten and threatened with assassination. On top of that, William's health started rapidly declining. He got painful ulcers and his vision got even worse.

Still, he kept trying, and finally, three days before he died, the Slavery Abolition Act passed the House of Commons. His lifelong goal achieved, William died a happy man.

- What is your goal in life?
- Who first told you about Jesus?

David Wilkerson

1931–2011 • United States

David Wilkerson sat in his living room, flipping through the latest issue of *Life* magazine. He scanned over ads for new refrigerators, cigarettes, and some new kids' toy called the hula hoop. But then his eyes landed on a black-and-white photo of a group of teen boys, fists raised, in a gritty, urban setting. The headline read "Mass Murder Trial of a Teen-Age Gang."

The group, known as the Egyptian Dragons, were on trial for their lives after killing a fifteen-year-old boy with polio. They were, by all accounts, hopeless teen delinquents. But as he looked at their faces on the page, David felt the Holy Spirit tell him, *Go. Find these boys. Tell them God loves them.*

So this son and grandson of Pentecostal ministers, who grew up in a house full of Bibles and had been preaching since age fourteen, packed up and moved to New York City. He burst into the courthouse on the day of their trial and asked to speak to the judge on their behalf.

But the judge hadn't gotten the memo from the Holy Spirit, so he kicked Wilkerson out of the courthouse. A spectator in the audience snapped a photo of him, and he became known as "the pastor who interrupted the gang trial."

However, the gang members he eventually did meet simply knew him as that skinny, unflinching preacher who came into neighborhoods even the police were afraid to go to. When Nicky Cruz, leader of the Mau Maus gang, threatened to kill him, David told him that even if Nicky cut him into one thousand pieces, every piece would love him.

That moment changed Cruz's life. He said he realized then that God was looking for him, and God had found him through David Wilkerson. Nicky left the gang—and drugs—behind, and together, he and David built a network of centers to help other teens recover from drugs too. And now, sixty years later, the organization is still helping kids across the US overcome their addictions.

- Has God ever asked you to go somewhere that felt scary to you?
- Instead of thinking the worst about someone, how can you try to see what God sees in them?

Ron Williams

1940–2003 • Australia

I'm sure he'll be here soon, love." Ron Williams's wife, Diana, patted her daughter on the knee while she glanced at her watch. It had been four hours since Ron left to get help for their stalled-out car. They were in the middle of nowhere, and it was getting late. *Please, Lord, let him be okay*, she thought.

"There, Mommy!" Her daughter was pointing across the field, and Diana could see her husband, with his signature winsome smile across his face, carrying—of all things—a dead rabbit.

"Dinner!" he shouted gleefully, as Diana rolled her eyes and smiled.

Her husband's carefree spirit was what she loved about him, but since the moment of his very premature birth his life had been a struggle. His Aboriginal mixed-race background made him the target of horrible pranks, and he was a school dropout at age fourteen. Then his grandfather—the only dad he'd ever known—was killed in an act of violence. Ron, riddled with guilt and grief, began to rebel.

But then, through a chance meeting with one of Ron's old friends, Jesus found him. The friend handed Ron a Bible and a painting of Jesus holding a lamb. Ron was overcome with emotion. He felt that the lamb represented his helplessness in life, and he decided to let Jesus take control.

From that day, he traveled thousands of miles through Australia's outback to share God's love. For many of these people, Christianity had been the "white man's" religion. But Ron made sure they knew that Jesus's love was meant for them too.

He believed money should be given away to those who needed it more than he did, and everything his little family owned was stored in the back of their car. Even though he didn't own fancy things, he was as comfortable visiting diplomats and jetsetters as he was with prisoners and drunks. And everywhere he went, his winsome smile, gentle disposition, and unswerving Christian faith changed lives.

Where once people had no hope, they found hope through Ron's message of God's love to people who thought, just maybe, God had forgotten about them.

- What's one way you know God loves you?
- How do other people know you love Jesus?

LOUIS Zamperini

1917–2014 • United States

"Finally!" Louis yelled when he spotted the American search plane, just a small blip in the vast blue sky above the Pacific. He and two crewmates had been afloat in the Pacific for days with no food, water, or hope. They were weak and exhausted, but they rallied to wave at the plane, thinking they were about to be rescued.

But there was no such luck for the marooned soldiers. The plane passed right by them. Though they were devastated, they were determined to survive, fighting off sharks with an oar and eating raw fish out of the ocean. As if things weren't bad enough, one of the men died after a couple of weeks of drifting.

When they finally made it to shore, Louis and his crewmate were immediately captured and thrown into a Japanese prisoner of war camp where they were tortured and half-starved. But Louis was strong and athletic; he'd even run track at the Olympics as a younger man. He used his stamina to help encourage the other POWs.

When Louis was finally released from captivity at the end of World War II, he was treated like a hero. But he didn't feel like a hero. Louis was haunted by his experiences at sea and in the POW camp. He started drinking heavily to keep his mind off his trauma.

Then one day his new wife attended a rally where Billy Graham spoke. She responded to God's quiet tug on her heart, becoming a Christian during the event and then encouraging Louis to do the same.

Accepting Jesus transformed Louis's life. Before, he'd struggled with bitterness and hatred toward his former captors, but now he visited them and offered them his forgiveness, no strings attached. Some of them even became Christians because they wanted to know the freedom and lightness Louis had.

And they weren't the only ones inspired by Louis. His story, which once seemed so hopeless, became a bestselling book and popular movie that's inspired millions of people around the world.

- Is there anyone in your life you need to forgive?
- Have you ever felt like you were lost or drifting? How did you find your way?

sources

Here are some of the books and websites that were used for research, which have more information on the men featured in *Stand-Up Guys*.

BOOKS

Brother Andrew with John and Elizabeth Sherrill. *God's Smuggler: Expanded Edition*. South Bloomington, Minnesota: Chosen Books, 2015.

Carpenter, Humphrey. *Tolkien: A Biography*. New York: Ballantine Books, 1977.

Coleman Holmes, Stuart. *Eddie Would Go: The Story of Eddie Aikau, Hawaiian Hero and Pioneer of Big Wave Surfing*. New York: St. Martin's Press, 2007.

Finster, Howard. *Howard Finster: Man of Visions*. Atlanta, GA: Peachtree Publishers, 1989.

Hamilton, Duncan. *For the Glory: Eric Liddell's Journey from Olympic Champion to Modern Martyr*. New York: Penguin Press, 2016.

Hardwick, Lamar. *I Am Strong: The Life and Journey of an Autistic Pastor*. Little Elm, TX: eLectio Publishing, 2017.

Harrison, Scott. *Thirst: A Story of Redemption, Compassion, and a Mission to Bring Clean Water to the World*. New York: Currency, 2018.

Hillenbrand, Laura. *Unbroken: An Olympian's Journey from Airman to Castaway to Captive (The Young Adult Adaptation)*. New York: Ember, 2017.

Jeung, Russell. *At Home in Exile: Finding Jesus among My Ancestors and Refugee Neighbors*. Grand Rapids, MI: Zondervan, 2016.

McMurry, Linda O. *George Washington Carver: Scientist and Symbol*. New York: Oxford University Press, 1981.

Paton, John G. and James Paton. *John G. Paton: Missionary to the New Hebrides: an Autobiography*. New York: Fleming H. Revell Company, 1907.

Paton, Mary Whitecross, and James Paton. *Letters and Sketches from the New Hebrides*. London: Hodder and Stoughton, 1905.

Smith, Father Jeremiah J. *Saint Maximilian Kolbe: Knight of the Immaculata*. Charlotte, NC: TAN Books, 1951.

Wilkerson, David, with John and Elizabeth Sherrill. *The Cross and the Switchblade*. New York: Berkley Books, 1986.

WEBSITES AND ONLINE ARTICLES

"About Fred." Biographical overview of Fred Rogers' life provided by Fred Rogers Center. www.fredrogerscenter.org/about-us/about-fred

Andrés, José. "When Natural Disasters Strike, Chef José Andrés Works Culinary Miracles for the Hungry." *Guideposts*, July 26, 2018. www.guideposts.org/inspiration/people -helping-people/when-natural-disasters-strike -chef-jos-andr-s-works-culinary

"Aristides de Sousa Mendes: His Life and Legacy." Sousa Mendes Foundation. sousamendesfoundation.org/aristides -de-sousa-mendes-his-life-and-legacy

Barrett, Paul. "Bryan Stevenson's Death-Defying Acts." *NYU Law Magazine*, Fall 2007. Posted online September 15, 2011. blogs.law.nyu.edu/magazine/2007/ bryan-stevenson's-death-defying-acts

Butler, Joey, and Mike DuBoise. "Appalachian Trail chaplain nears end of '2,200 miles of ministry.'" UM News, November 1, 2017. www.umnews.org/en/news/appalachian -trail-chaplain-nears-end-of-2200-miles-of -ministry

Copp, Jay. "The Nagasaki Martyrs." *Our Sunday Visitor*, July/August 1997, pages 25–28. Accessible online via www.catholicculture. org/culture/library/view.cfm?recnum=4024

Crowther, Samuel Ajayi. Letter to Reverend Williams Jowett, written in 1837. Originally published in *Patriot to the Core: Bishop Ajayi Crowther* by J. F. Ade-Ajayi. Accessible online via "Ajayi Crowther's 179-year old letter: My capture into slavery and rescue," *The News*, June 26, 2016. www.thenewsnigeria.com. ng/2016/06/ajayi-crowthers-179-year-old -letter-my-capture-into-slavery-and-rescue

Gonzales, Jason. "The 29-year-old hero from Waffle House shooting: 'I saw the opportunity and I took it.'" *The Tennessean*, April 24, 2018. www.tennessean.com/story/news/ crime/2018/04/22/waffle-house-shooting -hero-stopped-shooter/540061002

Haugen, Gary. "On a Justice Mission." *Christianity Today*, February 22, 2007. www.christianitytoday.com/ct/2007/ march/16.40.html

"John Lewis—March from Selma to Montgomery, 'Bloody Sunday,' 1965." National Archives—Southeast Region, Morrow, Georgia, Records of District Courts of United States. Eyewitness website. www.archives.gov/exhibits/ eyewitness/html.php?section=2

Quinn, Kenneth M., PhD. "Norman L. Borlaug—Extended Biography." World Food Prize, 2009. www.worldfoodprize.org/index. cfm?nodeID=87449&audienceID=1

"One Determined Dad . . . meet Pastor Lee Jong-rak." *Risen Magazine*, accessed August 6, 2019. www.risenmagazine.com/ pastor-lee-jong-rak

"Saint Oscar Arnulfo Romero." Franciscan Media. www.franciscanmedia.org/ saint-oscar-arnulfo-romero

Wayman, Sheila. "Why our elders are becoming environmental activists." *The Irish Times*, July 14, 2015. www.irishtimes.com/life-and-style/ health-family/parenting/why-our-elders-are -becoming-environmental-activists-1.2275470

"William Wilberforce." The Wilberforce School. www.wilberforceschool.org/about-us/ william-wilberforce

OTHER RESOURCES

Bombay Teen Challenge Ashagram (Kuniyal Kandi Devaraj): btcashagram.org

Border Angels (Enrique Morones): borderangels.org

Cecil and Iris Chaudhry Foundation (Cecil Chaudhry): ci-cf.org

Equal Justice Initiative (Bryan Stevenson): eji.org

Give Directly (Paul Niehaus and Michael Faye): givedirectly.org

International Justice Mission (Gary Haugen): ijm.org

The Red Road (Charles Robinson): theredroad.org

Show Hope (Steven Curtis Chapman): showhope.org

We Carry Kevan: wecarrykevan.com

World Central Kitchen (José Andrés): wck.org

ABOUT THE AUTHORS

Kate Etue is a freelance writer and a senior editor at CoolMomPicks.com. She lives with her husband and four children in Nashville, TN.

Caroline Siegrist is a creative writer based in Nashville, TN. She lives with her husband and son.